Made in the USA
Columbia, SC
25 January 2020

87130624R00057